The Question & Answer Book

ALL ABOUT
MOUNTAINS & VOLCANOES

SS1.4
m

ALL ABOUT MOUNTAINS & VOLCANOES

By Elizabeth Marcus

Illustrated by Joseph Veno

Troll Associates

Library of Congress Cataloging in Publication Data

Marcus, Elizabeth.
    All about mountains & volcanoes.

    (Question and answer book)
    Summary: Answers questions about the development of
mountains and volcanoes and about their influence on
the world's ecosystem and on human life.
    1. Mountains—Juvenile literature.   2. Volcanoes—
Juvenile literature.   [1. Mountains.   2. Volcanoes.
3. Earth sciences.   4. Questions and answers]
I. Veno, Joseph, ill.   II. Title.   III. Title: All
about mountains and volcanoes.   IV. Series.
GB512.M37   1984   551.4'32   83-4834
ISBN 0-89375-969-4
ISBN 0-89375-970-8 (pbk.)

Printed in the United States of America
10   9   8   7   6   5   4   3   2   1

What are the highest places on earth?

Mountains are the highest places on earth. Some mountains are so high that their tops seem lost in the clouds. Some are steep cliffs of jagged rock. Others look more like low, tree-covered hills.

What makes it a mountain?

No two mountains are exactly alike. But all mountains are alike in certain ways. A mountain rises at least 2,000 feet (610 meters) above the land that surrounds it. And a mountain has a rather narrow top called a *summit.* The *peak* is the highest point of the summit.

What is a mountain range?

Sometimes a mountain stands alone. More often, there are several mountains, called a *range*, fairly close together. A mountain range is usually much longer than it is wide. It may stretch out in a nearly straight line, or it may curve like a great hook. Some ranges have hundreds and hundreds of peaks. In the valleys and canyons between the peaks, there may be rivers and swiftly flowing streams.

Sometimes there are several mountain ranges in an area. They form a group of mountains called a *chain*.

What are submarine mountains?

When you think of mountains, you probably think of mountains that are on land. But many mountains are under water. They are called *submarine mountains,* and they stand on the ocean floor. If the peak of a submarine mountain is tall enough to stick out of the water, it forms an island.

Where is the longest chain of mountains?

The longest chain of mountains in the world is under water. This group of mountains is called the Mid-Atlantic Ridge. It runs down the middle of the Atlantic Ocean. The ridge stretches from Iceland in the north to the south Atlantic, where it branches out to the Pacific and Indian Oceans.

What is the altitude of a mountain?

The height or *altitude* of a land mountain tells how far its peak is above sea level. *Sea level* is the surface of the ocean. Of course, sea level changes with the tides. So the *average* sea level is used when the height of a mountain is measured.

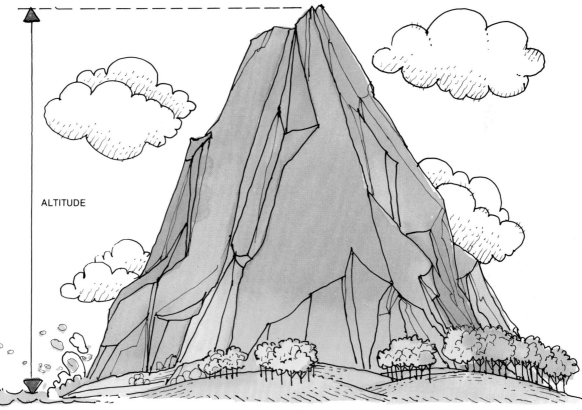

ALTITUDE

Surveyors are people who measure things. They use special instruments to find the height of a mountain. They can find the true height of a mountain without actually climbing it. But they must be able to see the mountain's peak.

9

Which is the highest mountain?

Mount Everest, in the Himalaya mountain range of south-central Asia, is the world's highest mountain. It is 29,028 feet (8,848 meters) high. Many have tried to climb Mount Everest, but in 1953 the first climbers succeeded. They were Sir Edmund Hillary of New Zealand and Tenzing Norgay of Nepal.

What is it like the higher you go?

If you have ever climbed a mountain, you may have noticed that the higher you went, the cooler the air became. These changing temperatures are one reason why different types of plants grow at different places on a mountain.

What plants grow on a mountain?

Plant growth is the same at the bottom of a mountain as on the land nearby. Higher up, where the air is cooler, there are fewer and thinner plants and trees. Still higher, where the air is much cooler, the trees are much smaller, and the grasses are stubby. Finally, beyond the *timber line*, or tree line, it is too cold for any trees to grow. There may be only bare rock, or this part of a mountain may be covered with ice and snow much or all of the year.

What is the snow line?

Above the *snow line* on a mountain, the snow never melts. The snow line can begin at different heights depending on how cold the climate is. In the Rocky Mountains, the snow line is about 2 miles (3 kilometers) above sea level. In Greenland, where the climate is colder, it is less than half a mile (.8 kilometer) above sea level. In the Arctic, the snow line is right at sea level.

How much rain falls on a mountain?

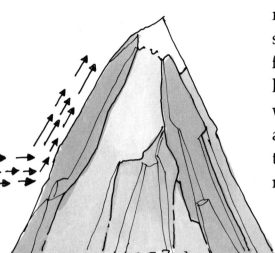

Different parts of a mountain receive different amounts of rain and snow. Currents of moist air blow in from the sea and sweep across the land. But a mountain is like a huge wall, blocking the path of the moving air. Since the air cannot go through the "wall," it begins to rise up the mountainside.

As air rises, it cools. And when air cools, it loses moisture, in the form of rain and snow. This moisture, called *precipitation*, falls on the side of the mountain that faces the wind. This is called the *windward* side. So the windward side of a mountain usually gets a lot of rain and snow.

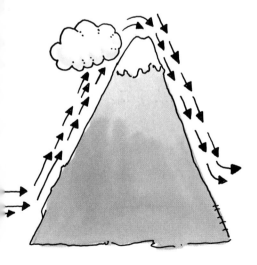

By the time the wind moves down the *leeward* side, or opposite side, of the mountain, it is a current of dry air. So the leeward side of a mountain usually has very little precipitation.

13

Why are mountains where they are?
How do mountains form?

Geologists, scientists who study the earth, say that mountains are caused by changes in the earth's *crust*. The crust is the outside layer of material that covers the earth like a thin skin. The land and the ocean floor are part of the earth's crust. Beneath the earth's crust are three other layers—the mantle, the outer core, and the inner core.

The earth's crust is broken into several rigid pieces, or *plates*. These plates "float" on the earth's mantle. Currents of hot rock in the mantle move beneath the earth's crust, carrying the plates along. The plates move, drifting very slowly—perhaps as little as a half inch (1.3 centimeters) each year. The very large areas of land, called *continents*, and the ocean floor are on top of the plates, so they drift, too—as if they were on floating rafts.

CONTINENTAL PLATE

CONTINENTAL PLATE

What does all this have to do with mountains? As huge, heavy land masses move, enormous pressures are created. And when two plates collide or scrape past one another, the great pressure can actually create mountains.

What are the four kinds of mountains?

There are four main kinds of mountains—folded mountains, block or faultblock mountains, dome mountains, and volcanic mountains. The names of these mountains have to do with the way they were created.

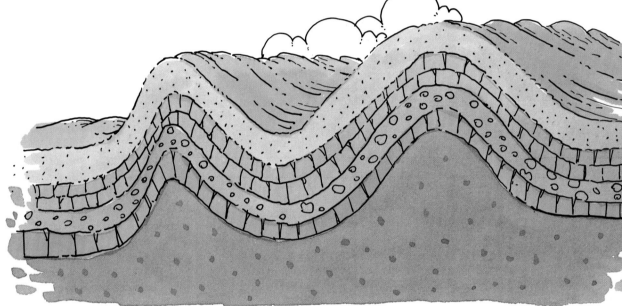

What are folded mountains?

The Appalachians of North America are examples of *folded mountains.* They were formed about 200 million years ago. Scientists think the plate carrying North America collided with the plate carrying Africa. The collision pushed the edge of the North American plate into great wrinkles or folds. These folded layers were forced upward and became the Appalachian Mountains.

What are block mountains?

The Sierra Nevada Mountains of eastern California are examples of *block* or *faultblock* mountains. Mountains like these are formed when the earth's crust breaks into blocks instead of folding. Some of the blocks move down, while others move up and become mountains.

What are dome mountains?

Sometimes, instead of folding or breaking, the earth's crust swells up into a great blister. It fills with hot, liquid rock called *magma*, which cools and hardens into a shape that looks like the top of a huge bubble. This is called a *dome* mountain. It is the way the Black Hills of South Dakota were formed.

17

What are volcanic mountains?

Lava, or magma that breaks through the earth's crust, can form another kind of mountain. Sometimes great pressure causes the earth's crust to crack or split. Lava pours up through the crack and piles higher and higher. In time, the cooled and hardened lava forms a mountain. Mount Vesuvius in Italy was formed this way. It is a *volcanic mountain*, or *volcano*.

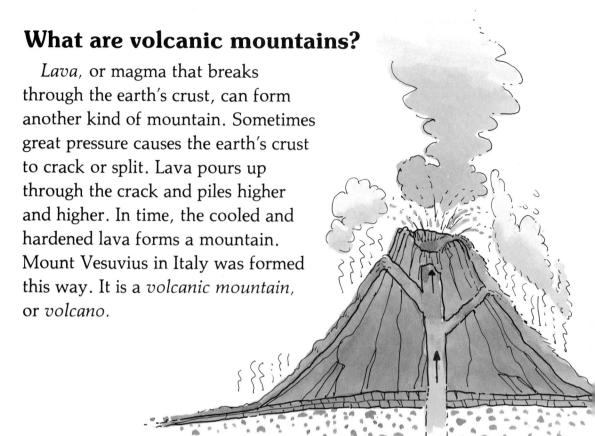

How does a volcano form an island?

Many volcanoes are under the ocean. If they grow high enough to stick out of the water, they form volcanic islands. Each of the eight main islands that make up the state of Hawaii is the top of a volcano. But only two of Hawaii's volcanoes still erupt. Mauna Loa erupts from time to time, sending streams of lava down to the sea. Kilauea erupts more often. A road has been built to the edge of the Kilauea crater, so people sometimes call it the "drive-in volcano."

What sorts of volcanoes are there?

Scientists divide volcanoes into groups, depending on how often they erupt. Some volcanoes are *extinct*, or dead. As far as we know, they no longer erupt at all. There are many extinct volcanoes all over the world. Mount Kilimanjaro—the highest point in Africa—is an extinct volcano.

Some volcanoes have not been "dead" long enough for us to be sure they will not erupt at some future time. Scientists call them *dormant*, or sleeping, volcanoes. Mount Fuji in Japan is a dormant volcano.

If a volcano erupts "every once in a while," it is said to be *intermittent*. Mount Etna in Sicily erupts often enough to be called an intermittent volcano.

But some volcanoes erupt regularly. Stromboli in Italy is often aglow with fire. This type of volcano is said to be *active*.

Many people picture a volcano's eruption as a great explosion of leaping, roaring fire and swooshing gases. But most volcanoes don't erupt that violently. Instead of spitting lava furiously into the air, they quietly push it out the top, where it hardens or flows slowly down the mountain slopes.

Did you ever see a volcano erupt?

If you did, you were watching a mountain grow. Each layer of lava and ash added to the size of the volcanic mountain, making it just a little higher or larger.

21

How does a mountain grow smaller?

Mountains of all kinds are always growing smaller. Erosion wears them down. *Erosion* is the wearing away of the earth's surface by the forces of the weather—wind, ice, and water.

Almost as soon as a mountain rises, erosion starts to wear it down. Rain and melting snow form streams, which lead into rivers. The flowing water slowly cuts channels in the rock, washing away stones and other material. Sometimes the rivers cut great canyons between mountain peaks.

If a mountain is very high, it may be so cold that snow and ice do not melt. If the ice becomes thick enough, it may form an ice river, or a *glacier*, and move down the mountain.

Glaciers move very slowly—perhaps only a few inches a day. But they cause a great deal of erosion. The heavy ice scrapes over the mountainside, making rough slopes smoother and carving deep valleys.

23

Erosion is at work on all mountains—on old ones, like the Appalachians, and on younger ones, like the Rockies. The older a mountain range is, the more time erosion has had to do its work. That is why the peaks of a very old mountain range tend to be smoother and rounder than those of a range that is younger. It may seem hard to believe, but someday the rough and rugged Rocky Mountains will look very much like the rounded peaks of the Appalachians. Erosion will have done its job.

How much of the earth is covered by mountains?

Mountains cover about a fifth of the world's land. Except for the high peaks of eastern Africa, most of the major land mountains form two great mountain systems, called *bands*.

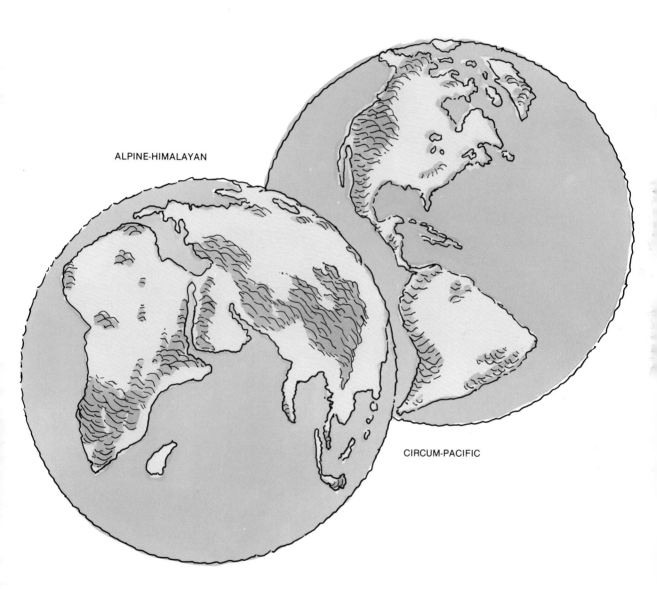

ALPINE-HIMALAYAN

CIRCUM-PACIFIC

The Alpine-Himalayan band runs east-west across Europe and Asia, covering about 6,000 miles (9,600 kilometers). The other band is called the *circum-Pacific system*, because it circles the Pacific Ocean.

Why are mountains important?

URANIUM
COAL TIN
COPPER GOLD
SILVER IRON

People like to climb mountains, vacation on them, and simply admire their beauty. But mountains are also important for other reasons. Rich deposits of coal, iron, copper, tin, uranium, salt, gold, silver, and precious rocks and minerals often lie beneath the surface of a mountain. People mine these materials by digging into the mountainsides.

Thin soil and steep slopes make many mountains poor places to farm. But in countries where land is scarce, people do farm the mountainsides. In China and Southeast Asia, farmers build step-like terraces to hold the soil on the slopes.

In other areas, the volcanic ash that covers the sides of volcanic mountains is rich and fertile. Farmers in places like Indonesia plant their crops in this fertile soil, even though a new eruption could suddenly bury everything under molten lava.

What else do mountains give us?

The great forests that grow on many mountainsides give us lumber. Rich mountain grasslands are used for grazing. As the grass in the valleys grows dry and brown in the sun, people move their herds into the hills, where the animals can find fresh grass and clear water.

The rivers and streams that rush down steep mountain slopes provide water power for electricity. Large dams and power plants have been built on several mountain rivers.

Mountains are also the homes of wild animals, including snow leopards, bears, giant pandas, goats, and sheep. The high, faraway mountain peaks on which these animals live help to keep them safe from hunters and other enemies.

Long ago, people were afraid of mountains. Instead of bears or leopards, they thought that witches or dragons lived there. Today, we know a great deal about the mountains of the world. We have climbed to the top of the highest mountain peaks. We have built highways and railroads on mountainsides. Towns and cities have been built on mountain slopes. We go to the mountains to hike, to camp, and to ski. We drive through them, fly over them, and dig into them. We gaze up at their towering heights and wonder at their majesty. For each mountain is, in its own special way, a very unique and beautiful part of nature.